My Lost Top

Written by Diane Engles

Illustrated by John Jones

I had a top.

It was a fast top.

4

It was the best top.

But one day the top just did not stop.

It slid past my dad.

It slid past my mom.

It went so fast.

It did not stop.

It hit the door with a snap.

But it still did not stop.

It went down the step.

It must be lost.

Too bad.

It was my best top.

16